A BAD HAIR DAY IS A GOOD HAT DAY:

Secrets to a Simpler Life.

by Dee Ann Stewart

DESIGN: MARK EIMER; PHOTOGRAPHY: TODD BALFOUR,
WILLIAM KRZYZANOWSKI; DIGITAL IMAGING: TODD BALFOUR

After you've eaten all the raw cookie dough, you might as well turn off the oven.

Be a really good driver.
It will throw men off.

Plan your
ironing around a
made-for-TV movie.

You can't kill
dried flowers.

Try to be the one woman who looks better after an in-store make over.

If you're going
antique hunting,
prepare yourself for
some odd smells.

Set a new record
for the longest time
without balancing
your checkbook.

Listen to a song
that reminds you of
someone nice.

Visit your parents and drink from the carton.

Don't refluff the guest towels — just admit that you used them.

Find the cure for the
ice-cream headache.

Keep waving
even after you've
realized the person
you're waving to
isn't who you
thought it was.

Skip your vitamins
just to see what
happens.

If you're not crafty,
don't make crafts.

Don't name
your children after
characters in
romance novels.

Knowing the shape
of your face is not the
key to happiness.

Amuse yourself with the "prom issue" of a fashion magazine.

See how many days
you can go
without shaving.

Take out all the
stiff cardboard inserts
before you sit down to
read a magazine.

If you get colored
contacts, make sure
it's a color that
exists in nature.

Force yourself
to wear one of the
hats you bought and
never wear.

Wear your underwear
with the good
waistband today.

Watch a man
fold clothes.

Try to sneeze
before you put on
your mascara.

Shop in a store where
a smaller size will fit.

If you find someone
with your dream hair,
                tell them.

Never check the
fat content on a
candy bar.

See how long you can actually wear a pair of thong underwear.

Be the one person who's found a second use for a bridesmaid's dress.

Rent a movie starring
the actress people say
you look like.

If bugs make a
permanent home
in your hair spray,
you may be wearing
too much.

If you don't know
the ending to a joke,
don't start it.

Remember, ice-cream
trucks don't take
credit cards.

Play hangman using
dirty words.

Don't try to drink
anything while
watching
home movies.

Cheese popcorn is not
a dairy product.

Torture the roof of your mouth with some kid cereal.

Help a Boy Scout
cross the street.

Don't be the person who has a special order at a fast-food restaurant.

Try to look graceful
while putting on a
sports bra.

Don't get jealous
when you receive
a postcard.

Try to make a
pitcher of lemonade
without choking on
lemonade dust.

Order the jumbo
popcorn or none
at all.

Play with a baby's face
while it's sleeping.

Don't mistake an inviting pile of leaves for a compost pile.

Write something
more clever than
"Wash me!"
on a dirty car.

Don't lose sleep over which long distance company to use.

Flush while someone's
in the shower.

Refuse to make
a call from a
touch-tone phone.

Try to unwrap a
baked potato without
rolling the tinfoil
into a ball.

Wear your hair
the way people tell
you they like it.

Try to figure out what
makes nonfat cheese
taste so bad.

Remember:
A bad hair day is a
good hat day.

Use high fashion as a guide and then bring it down to earth.

Try not to
get depressed when
shopping with
rich friends.

Send your kids
to school with lipstick
on their cheeks.

Start making up
excuses now for
not flossing.

Try not to see a
movie theater floor
in broad daylight.

Don't count
other people's items
in the express lane.

Try on a friend's
glasses and admit it
if you see better.

Watch people
race walking and
try not to smile.

It's OK if you throw
like a girl.

Leave a big enough lipstick stain so no one drinks after you.

Use silly voices
when you read a book
to your kids.

Don't pretend to shop before you head straight for the sale rack.

Make sure you have
ice cream before
sitting down to pay
your bills.

It takes a really good imagination not to get bored on a stair climber after three minutes.

Notice how
class reunions
never include a
pool party.

If a recipe calls
for a double boiler,
turn the page in the
cookbook.

Visit a school
and swing on the
swing set.

Establish a junk drawer before you even move in.

Tell a pregnant
woman she's
"all baby."

Hair color
changes your looks,
not your life.

Visit truck stops and buy up all the silver naked ladies.

Don't confuse bug
spray with any other
spray you might use.

The baby crying
on the plane is not
purposely trying to
ruin your life.

Try to find the one
hairdresser who has
normal hair.

Seeing foreign films
doesn't make you
smart.

Fight the urge
to make your bed
at a hotel.

If you don't have kids,
don't go places where
they eat for free.

Pictures next to recipes are only suggestions.

A big ruffle at the top
of your swimsuit
can only do so much.

All the showers in romantic movies are bigger than yours.

Buy a gift for a teacher
that has nothing to do
with apples.

Not noticing your haircut doesn't mean he doesn't care.

Take your mom
to see a girl movie.

Keep the good scissors
hidden at all times.

No dessert is
too pretty to eat.

Don't stop singing
with the car radio
at red lights.

It takes a confident person to use the magnified side of the makeup mirror.

If someone asks what team you play for, your shoulder pads may be too big.

Find a way to get
vacuum lines in your
carpet without actually
vacuuming.

It doesn't count
as a stain if you can
tuck it in.